BEACON PRESS   BOSTON

Arthur B. Mazmanian

THE STRUCTURE OF PRAISE

A DESIGN STUDY
ARCHITECTURE FOR RELIGION
IN NEW ENGLAND
FROM THE 17TH CENTURY TO THE PRESENT

Type: Helvetica
Composition: Wrightson Typographers
Paper: 70# Mohawk Novarra
Printing: Halliday Lithograph Co.
Binding: Colonial Press Inc.
Design and photographs: Arthur B. Mazmanian

3

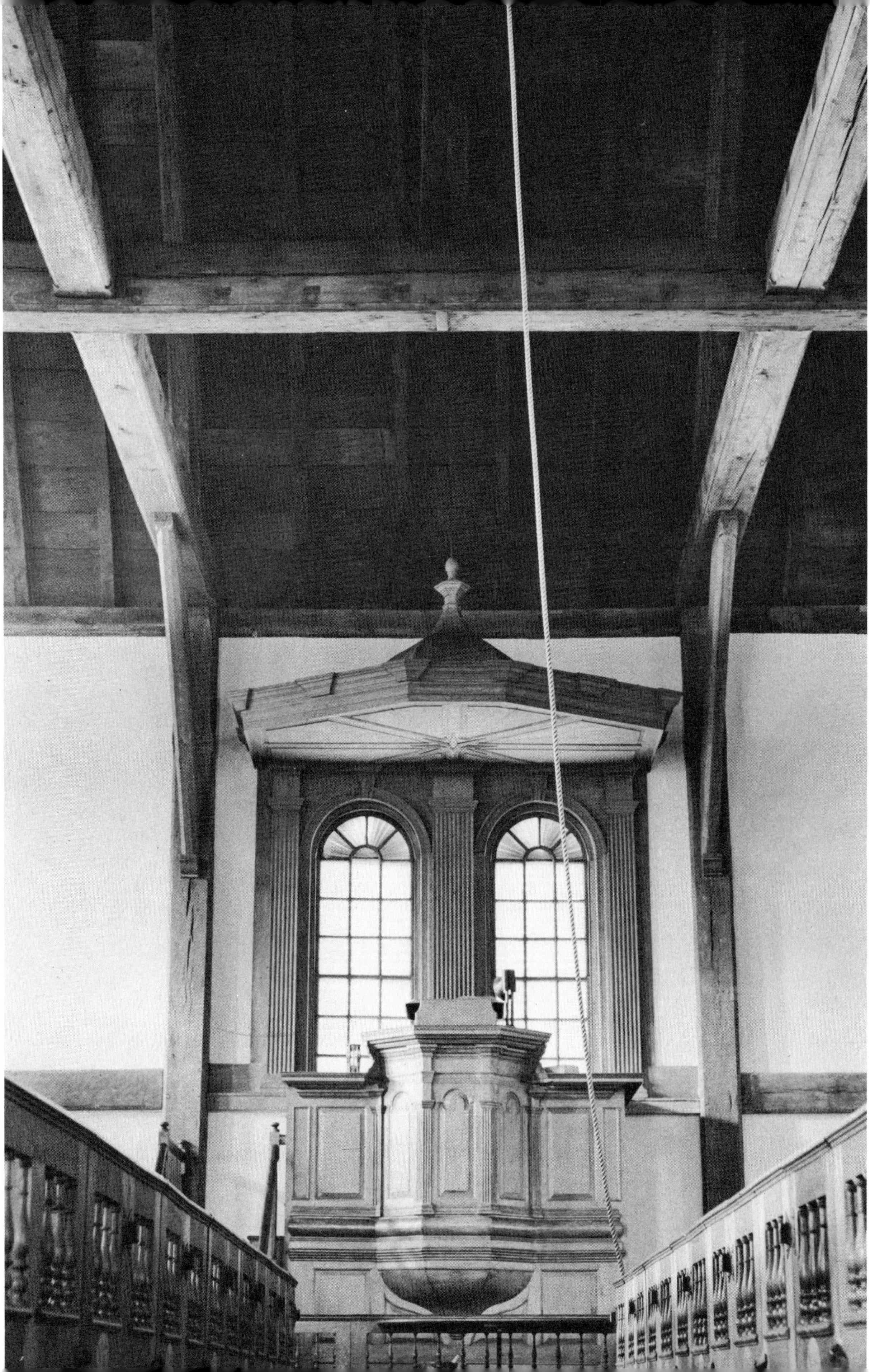

FOREWORD

The illustrations that follow are not arranged chronologically but by juxtaposing forms that either relate or contrast in an attempt to build a composition that will best express visually the nature of New England ecclesiastical architecture of the last 300 years. This format is used to accomplish two goals: To celebrate the architectural achievements of a small but influential region, and to suggest to the layman that there are architects and designers working today with the necessary insight, imagination, and skills to return some measure of order to the visual chaos of our communities.

The decision to include a building was not made on theological or historical grounds, but by using certain aesthetic criteria to judge how well the structure took its place in its environment. It is hoped that the nature of these criteria will be revealed by the forms themselves through the photographs and their organization in the book, with an assist from the accompanying text. It will become quite obvious that the choices are very personal ones made by one who, although not an architect, is involved in form-making. Some liberties were taken in the graphic presentation of the buildings in order to find a language that would transfer a large three-dimensional object to the minute two-dimensional surface of a page. The intent is to re-create in some measure the actual experience of a building.

Old Ship Meetinghouse, the earliest (1681) as well as the first to appear in these pages, leads because it precisely exhibits the qualities valued in structures to follow. The understanding of materials and their honest use, the forms dictated by necessity, the controlled complexity of parts like the loft, the general disregard for pretension, the retention of a basic simplicity despite changes and additions, all combine to make it an extraordinary building, a special place.

1681 Old Ship Meetinghouse. Unitarian. The First Parish of Hingham, Massachusetts.
1) View from southwest.   2) Pulpit windows in the northwest wall.   3) Pulpit and pews from the eighteenth century. 4, 5) The underside of the roof with its supporting beams and trusses. Old Ship Meetinghouse, the oldest frame house of worship in America, was completed during the winter of 1681–2. For nearly 100 years, until 1780, it served for town meetings as well as for worship.

7 1966 *Unitarian Universalist Church.*
Andover, Massachusetts. Joseph J. Schiffer,
architect. The concrete section appearing in the
exterior approach backs the open arrangement
of the organ pipes.

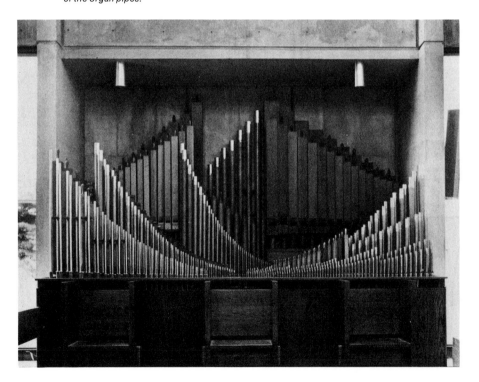

This Stone is erected in Memory of Miss Ann Mercy Brewer, who was born in New-Port Rhode-Island Sep[t]. 21. A.D. 1736. She lived a life of piety and virtue & died January 1st A.D. 1789 in the Joyfull expectation

8 1770 Trinity Church. Anglican. Brooklyn, Connecticut. Godfrey Malbone, designer. (See 116.)

9 1759–63 Touro Synagogue. Congregation Jeshuat Israel. Newport, Rhode Island. Peter Harrison, architect. Buff painted brick with brown trim.   10 Entrance porch with arches and Ionic columns.

Peter Harrison (1716–1775)

Touro Synagogue (9, 10), Christ Church (11), and King's Chapel (12) were built from the designs of Peter Harrison of Rhode Island. He arrived in Newport from England in 1738 and became a merchant in the busy seaport. Although in commerce throughout his life, as an amateur architect he designed some of the important buildings of the Colonial period. He apparently derived architectural knowledge from the excellent collection of pattern books he acquired; among them were Campbell's *Vitruvius Britannicus*, Hoppus' *Palladio*, and Gibbs' *The Book of Architecture*. The handsome structures included here are a result of his intelligent use of details from these books in forms that meet new requirements.

The three Harrison buildings, all for worshipers outside the prevailing Puritan tradition, have interiors of considerable richness. The exteriors, however, are notable for their restraint. The impression of understatement is suggested by contrasting the complexity and ornament in the porticoes and window shapes with the simple forms of the structures. The exaggeration of some parts as points of reference, the introduction of the intricate in the midst of the severe, the juxtaposition of the mature with the nascent, are among the elements Harrison used to create exceptional form.

11   1761   Christ Church. Anglican. Cambridge, Massachusetts.
Peter Harrison, architect. The exterior is wood, painted gray.

12   1749–54   King's Chapel. Unitarian. Originally Anglican. Boston,
Massachusetts. Peter Harrison, architect. The Ionic portico around the
tower was added about 1790. The building is of Quincy granite.

13 1802–4 St. Stephen's Roman Catholic Church. Originally Congregational. Boston, Massachusetts. Charles Bulfinch (1763–1844), architect. Recently restored.

14 1820 The Cathedral Church of St. Paul. Anglican. Boston, Massachusetts. Alexander Parris (1780–1852) and Solomon Willard (1788–1861), architects.

15 1826 Johnson Chapel. Amherst College. Amherst, Massachusetts. Isaac Damon (1781–1862), architect.

16 1816 First Church of Christ Unitarian. Lancaster, Massachusetts. Charles Bulfinch, architect.   17   Detail of horse sheds.

The two Greek Revival churches, St. Paul's and the Johnson Chapel, and the two Bulfinch designs, St. Stephen's and Christ Church, were all constructed within a twenty-five year period in the early nineteenth century. The four buildings are impressive in size and character, each suggesting the wealth and importance of its congregation. They also demonstrate a change in style taking place about 1820. The Bulfinch churches display the delicacy and lightness of detail characteristic of the Adamesque-Federal style adapted from classical Roman models, while the two later structures reveal the restraint and formality inherent in the Greek-temple form. The gradual realization that Greece rather than Rome was the source of classical culture and the fact that the new American Republic found it easier to identify politically with ancient Greece than with imperial Rome led to the Greek Revival which dominated all types of building until the Civil War period.

The dignity and composure of St. Paul's (14) is so unexpected in its noisy, congested locale that one is startled when first noticing it. Amherst Chapel (15), on the other hand, occupies a commanding position amidst similar buildings on a quiet college campus.

16

18   1964 Unitarian Church.
Westport, Connecticut. Victor A.
Lundy, architect. Rising from a
densely wooded ridge is this
fantastic, hovering roof made of
hundreds of 2 x 4's nailed side by
side on edge and running the long
dimension of the building. The deck
is supported by widely spaced,
heavy, laminated wood arches.

19   View into sanctuary. The
structure is a highly emotional form
created by pairing a wild, natural
site with an uninhibited but knowing
imagination.

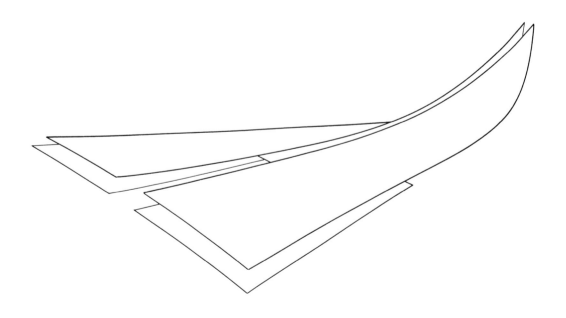

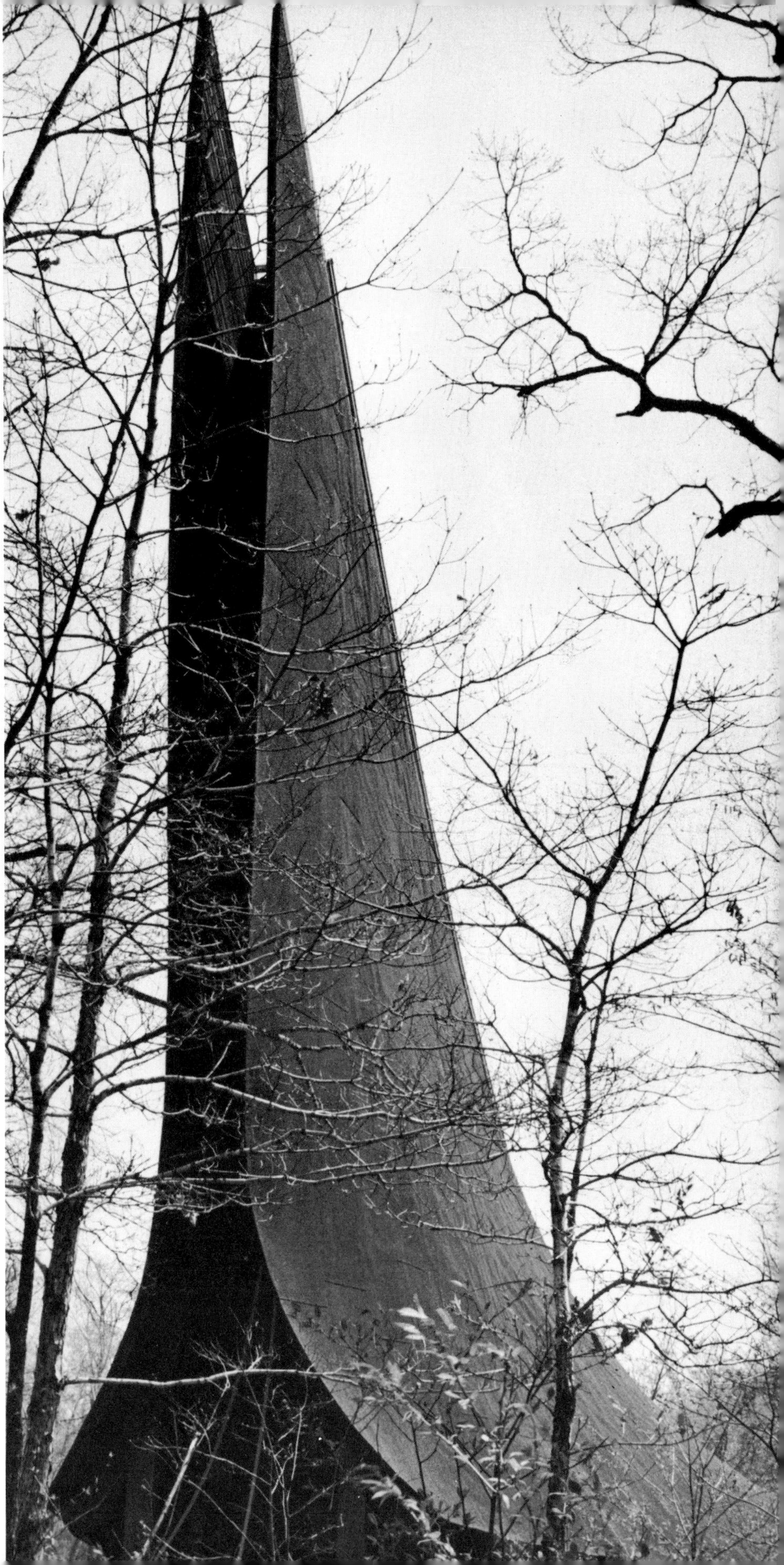

20 1962 United Church of Christ. West Norwalk, Connecticut. Victor Christ-Janer, architect. The triangular forms which enclose the church are neoprene-covered plywood panels joined together with a steel frame.

21   1969 Presbyterian Church of Old Greenwich. Old Greenwich,
Connecticut. Richard E. Schoenhardt, Galliher and Schoenhardt,
architect. Through the courtyard, left above, is the main entrance to the
sanctuary. The curved wall adjoining the sanctuary forms a small chapel
for ecumenical use.

22   1963 Our Lady of Jasna Gora Church. Clinton, Massachusetts. Henneberg and Henneberg, architects. Built for a predominantly Polish congregation, this Catholic Chuch contains design elements recalling the Middle Ages. The medieval church, placed on a hill high above the town, was often used for defense as well as for worship (e.g., the crossbowmen used the narrow windows to ward off attackers). The two domed side-chapels are reminiscent of the Polish practice of building numerous chapels off the main body of the church to honor various saints. The entrance wall displays a highly developed iconography. The brightly colored bricks around the doorway form images found in the catacombs. The figures and colors, the Grecian Cross, the height of the wall itself, all have symbolic meanings. These have created a rather surprising edifice in an ordinary manufacturing town.

23   1966 Church of the Resurrection. Roman Catholic. Wallingford, Connecticut. Russell, Gibson, and von Dohlen, architects. Oiled copper roof and fascia with red brick walls. The structure grows from a slight rise in a large open field. The builders of the developing community around this large (900-seat) church could learn much from its simple, unpretentious form. The two side walls, similar in form, have a slight curve along their lengths.

IAM NON ES
ET ADVENAE
CIVES SANC
DOMESTICI
AEDIFICATIS
MENTVM AP
ET PROPHET
SVMMIAN CV
CHRISTO
QVO OMNIS
CONSTRVCTA
TEMPLVM S
DOMINO +
CO AEDIFICA
BITACVLVM D

24   1960 The Church and Monastery for Portsmouth Priory. Rhode Island. Pietro Belluschi; Anderson, Beckwith, and Haible, associated architects. The church serves both the community of Benedictine monks and the Portsmouth Priory School.

25

26   27

Religion and art are both a search for truth, which is forever eluding, forever challenging, never fully possessed, only intuitively felt, and the very essence of God's mystery. The fruits of this continuous search, when made in earnest and not by repeating worn-out formulas, carry the deepest and the most desirable meaning through the ages. — Pietro Belluschi*

25   *The copper entrance doors of the church. Designed by Dom Peter Sidler and John T. Benson and executed by Dom Peter Sidler. The text in Latin is Ephesians 11:19 — 22.   26   View of the nave and the altar, with the retro-choir beyond. The wire sculpture above the altar is the work of Richard Lippold.*

27   *The site is a hillside overlooking Narragansett Bay.*

28   *1967 Science building of the Priory School. Pietro Belluschi; Robinson, Green, and Beretta, associated architects.*

The inclusion in a book of religious buildings of the Priory School's science building and of the Shaker barn on the following page is justified because they serve religious communities. More importantly, they are presented here along with an office building (144) because to those prepared to respond to the emotional possibilities of form, their presence evokes a deeply felt spiritual experience.

*Quoted from Recent American Synagogue Architecture, catalog of an exhibition at the Jewish Museum, New York, 1963.

THE DANCE

29, 30   1826   *Circular stone barn. Hancock (Mas-*
sachusetts) Shaker Community. Rebuilt 1969.

31   *Shaker worship dance. Drawn by B. J. Lossing.*
From Harper's New Monthly Magazine *(July 1857).*
(A.A.S.)

The unusual round form of the great stone barn was utilized to conveniently allow hay wagons to drive
in a circle, unloading their hay. The wagons traveled the circuit on a level above the animals being fed.
This clearly articulated interior space, dominated by rafters fanning out from the central mast, is an
awe-inspiring sight.

   The meetinghouse on the following pages was moved to Hancock in 1962 from its original site at
Shirley in the central part of the state. It replaces an identical meetinghouse on the site that had been
built in 1785. Both were constructed by Moses Johnson of Enfield, New Hampshire, a Shaker who is
thought to have built at least seven similar houses in eastern Shaker communities.

   The two-story structure's exterior is patterned after buildings of the period in New England and in
the Hudson River Valley. The Shakers' doctrine of separation of the sexes made necessary such
changes as the additional doorway in the second level. The two sets of rooms on that level were the
living quarters and the offices of the two Elders and the two Eldresses who guided the community.
The front doors lead directly into a large room on the first floor where the Shakers worshiped and
performed their characteristic dances, songs, and rituals. This large, unobstructed space has
benches only along the walls. The woodwork is blue and the walls and exterior of the building are
white. The white exterior and gambrel roof were features reserved for the meetinghouse.

   The strict symmetry of Shaker design reflects a striving for simplicity and order in all functions of
life as well as the duplication demanded by separation of the sexes. Symmetrical form is also present
in the beautiful furniture and inspirational drawings of the society. The pen-and-ink "spirit"
drawings (75, 76) made during a period of religious fervor (1835–1855) were done by certain Shakers
acting as transmitters of messages or "gifts" from the spirit world. The elements in these intricate
drawings—trees, musical instruments, altars, stars, and fanciful architecture—are balanced on either
side of a central, vertical axis.

32 *1792–3 Shaker Meetinghouse. Hancock, Massachusetts. Moses Johnson, builder. The engraving, "Ring Dance, Niskeyuna," is from* Frank Leslie's Popular Monthly, *Vol. XX, No. 6, December 1885. (A.A.S.)*

33   *A detail of the large, unobstructed space used in Shaker worship.*

34   The two churches shown separately on the following pages appear
together in this photograph. On the left here and in 36 is Old Saint Mary's
Church. On the right and in 35 is Union Church.

35   1773 Union Church. Anglican. West Claremont, New Hampshire.
Tower and belfry 1800. The twenty-five-foot extension of the structure
in 1820 can be noted in the photograph by the slightly smaller size of the
two windows on the left.

36   1824 Old Saint Mary's Church. Roman Catholic. West Claremont,
New Hampshire. Virgil Barber, S.J., builder. The unevenness in the
brickwork in the side view (34) is a result of the removal of an extension
during recent restoration of the structure.

These two churches along the Connecticut River are, coincidentally, the oldest of their respective
faiths in New Hampshire. Union Church, built in a time of Congregational dominance, is outwardly
much like the simple, wooden, eighteenth-century New England meetinghouses. The only atypical
parts are the rounded tops of the windows and the entrance in the short side. The name "Union" is
said to have resulted from the joint venture of Anglicans and Congregationalists in building the church.
Apparently the union was not able to survive the Revolution; the Congregationalists withdrew.

Father Virgil Barber, the builder of Old Saint Mary's, was the son of a minister of Union Church.
Both he and his father, the Rev. Daniel Barber, converted to Catholicism. The unusual form of
Saint Mary's is most likely the result of the Barbers' familiarity with the architecture of the middle
colonies, and especially with strongly Catholic Maryland. The use of brick, the laying of the brick in
Flemish bond, the details around the windows and doorway, and the wood blinds, all recall building
practices common to Maryland. The dimensions of the building, the considerable height relative to its
width, have a marked resemblance to a canal house in Amsterdam or Bruges. However, the intent may
have been to express the builder's new faith by using the proportions, on a human scale, of the
Catholic cathedrals of Europe. The succinct form of Old Saint Mary's and the restraint shown in the
use of decoration are an indication of the designer's understanding of his resources in carrying out
such a plan. Later attempts to transplant inspired forms of the Middle Ages to America resulted in
affectations and theatricality because their adapters either ignored or were unable to recognize
the limits within which every designer must work.

38 1785 Rocky Hill Meetinghouse.
Amesbury, Massachusetts.
Timothy Palmer, builder. 37 Pul-
pit. 39 Interior.

40 Detail of View of Boston *by James Turner*
(—1759). *Woodcut from the* American Magazine,
July 1745. (A.A.S.)

41 1729 Old South Meetinghouse
*(Third Church, Congregational). Boston,
Massachusetts. Robert Twelves, designer.*

Old South differs in several respects from the typical
eighteenth-century meetinghouses encountered frequently
in these pages. Its size, so large that it was the largest meeting
place in Boston, the masonry construction of the walls, and the
rounded-headed windows are unlike the small-town meetinghouses that dot New England. In these details it is much more
like the slightly earlier Anglican Christ Church (Old North,
1723) nearby (128). The interior, both a witness and a victim of
much activity during the Revolutionary period, was arranged in
the more usual meetinghouse pattern which had the main
entrance and pulpit facing each other on the long sides of the
building. The handsome structure resulting from this
combination of influences seems quite capable of visually
outlasting the enormous, pretentious buildings that surround it.

I. This study is undertaken for those concerned with the quality of their environment and the development of a twentieth-century aesthetic. Although it focuses on one type of building, it is done with the realization that the character of an environment can be expressed only in terms of the interaction of many factors of varying importance. The total expression can be one of excitement, wonder, and great beauty.

The religious structure, because it has traditionally represented the beliefs and aspirations of communities, seems an ideal subject for examination. New England (42), because of its early and long settlement as an English colony, has many fine eighteenth- and nineteenth-century meetinghouses and churches and one excellent meetinghouse from the seventeenth century. In the twentieth century, great population shifts and expansion have created a need for hundreds of new churches and synagogues. Included here are the very few in New England that were judged successful both functionally and aesthetically as representative of worshipers of diverse needs.

The much-admired early meetinghouses and churches play an important part in a study concerned with developing a viable twentieth-century aesthetic. The necessity for the colonist to find new forms for his house of worship in a new environment is similar to a problem faced by modern man. In the light of rapidly

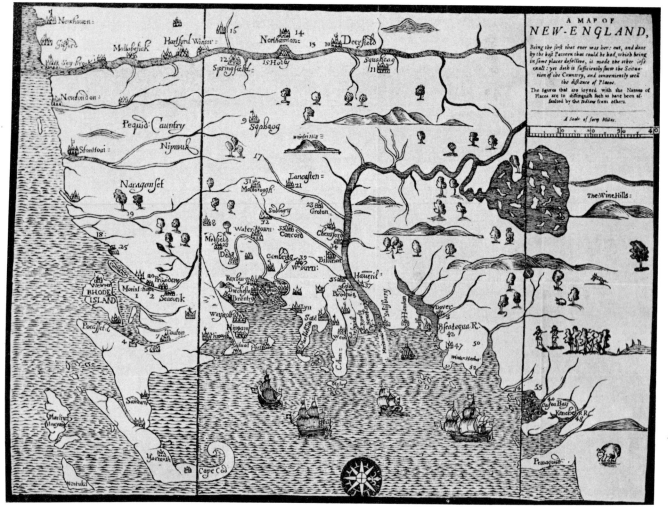

A MAP OF
NEW-ENGLAND,

Being the first that ever was here cut, and done by the best Pattern that could be had, which being in some places defective, it made the other less exact: yet doth it sufficiently shew the Scituation of the Country, and conveniently well the distance of Places.

The figures that are joyned with the Names of Places are to distinguish such as have been assaulted by the Indians from others.

A Scale of forty Miles.

10   20   30   40

Newhauen
Gifford
Wall Sey Brook
Mollabesick   Hartford Winsor   15   14   Northamton   13   10   Deerfield
                                 12   15 Hadly
                           Springfield   Squakeag
Newlondon   11

Pequid Country   9 Saphaog
            Nipmuk
                        17

Naragansef   31 the
                      Marlborough   Lancaster
                                     21
                   Sudbury   23 Groton
            19
   18:         Water-Town 32   Chensford
            25   Medfield   33 Concord   34
                      Dedham   Cambridg 35 Billricka
           20 Providence Roxbury   Woburn
Viewer Monnt hope   Dorchester Boston   Haueril
RHODE   1 2 Seaconk Brantry   55 Broford 37
ISLAND   Lyn
Pocasset   Weymoth   Sate
         7 Taulon   Nipuam
   4   5   Salual Haubn   Dover
                                                   Bscatequa R.
                                                   46
                                                   47   50
Martins   Winter Harbor
Vineyard   Sandwich   51   52

                                                              55
                                                        Cafco Bay
                                                        Kenebeck R.
                                                        48
Nantukt   Cape Cod   Pemaquid

The Wine Hills:

42

developing knowledge in science and technology, long-held values and traditions in both art and religion are being reassessed. Until quite recently, ecclesiastical architecture has ignored these challenges by escaping to romanticized versions of the past or denying that new possibilities exist.

A dependence on past styles was even more prevalent during most of the nineteenth century, not only in the United States, but generally throughout the Western world. The past has always been a useful source of information; how the information is used is the determining factor in any attempt at a critical evaluation of resulting forms:

> One way to use the past is to regard it as a useful dictionary from which one can select forms and shapes. The nineteenth century did this, using the past as a means of escape from its own time by masking itself with the shells of bygone periods.
>
> The fashion of the 1960s is more refined. It only flirts with the past, nibbling at random details—pointed arches, renaissance porticoes, cupolas—giving them a surrealistic flavoring, so as to achieve a "poetic" expression.
>
> The creative artists of this period have taken another way: poets,

42 A Map of New England *by John Foster (c. 1677). From the London edition of Hubbard's* Narrative of the Troubles with the Indians in New England. *(A.A.S.)*

painters, sculptors, and architects alike. In their work, past, present, and future merge together as the indivisible wholeness of human destiny.[1]

The confusion in religious architecture is a relatively recent phenomenon:

Until the sixteenth century religious building had been, for most civilizations, the important and dominant building of any city. At certain times all valuable architectural experimentation that was going on was part of church building programmes. The term "medieval architecture" recalls instantly the vaulting appropriate to a medieval church rather than that of any castle or palace.[2]

. . . all great churches in history were as "modern" for their time as possible. Their clergy and architects never dreamed of aping the past even when new additions were made onto old churches. Consider the two towers of Chartres, for instance, one emerging from the Romanesque, its neighbor handsomely expressing the full flower of the Gothic . . . in Italy scores of churches proclaim proudly, and rightly, the different additions which the centuries have bequeathed them.[3]

Church buildings, so much a part of everyone's environment, should regain their former position as leaders in architectural experimentation. Their function, which is both practical and spiritual, nearly affords the architect the freedom of invention of the sculptor or the painter. In the newer churches pictured, this freedom is evident in varying degrees. Often the buildings with the most un-expected forms seem also to be the ones that most clearly articulate their reason for being — a space in which a community of persons, with specific needs, gathers to worship.

This space, history has shown, can assume many forms:

> The earliest existing House of God may be such a wall-painted cave
> as the Font de Gaume in the Dordogne Valley or the Salle de Cartailhac
> of Tuc D'Audoubert. The cavern of Altamira, near Santander, with
> its "magical" hunting scenes painted or engraved on the walls and roof,
> may justly be regarded as the Sistine Chapel of Aurignacian or
> Magdalenian man . . . an early sanctuary was a clearing in the natural
> forest (43).[4]

The mysterious, beautifully arranged boulders of Stonehenge (44), the temples

43   *See 150 for a forest area deliberately set aside and maintained for worship.*
44   *Detail of Stonehenge. Salisbury Plain, England (c. 1500 B.C.).*

carved in the living rock of Egypt, the Greek Acropolis and Roman Pantheon, the tents of nomads, and the Temples of Solomon and Herod are but a few forms taken by the House of God in the pre-Christian era. These radically differing structures very clearly reflect solutions to many forms of worship. The techniques and materials utilized were the finest available to the builders. This pattern continues in any listing of the monuments of religious architecture.

> The form of a building . . . is not arbitrary but grows within the pattern
> of use, it is shaped by the movement people make inside it. The Church,
> therefore, took over certain architectural forms from the pagan world
> and used them to enclose analogous functions in the pattern of
> movement made by Christian worship.[5]

II. A description of the period that produced the meetinghouses and early churches of New England is important to the understanding of the architecture. The meetinghouse in the New England village housed both the religious life and the government of the community. The village itself consisted of a group of nearby farms. Proximity was desirable for several reasons. In the earliest settlements it afforded greater protection from Indian raids. In a day of few roads and slow

45 Divine Examples of God's Severe Judgements upon Sabbath Breakers. *Printed broadside with woodcuts. James Franklin (?), (1696–1735). From the collection of the Worcester Art Museum, Worcester, Massachusetts.*

transportation, being near the meetinghouse and various shops and stores was advantageous. Furthermore, it perhaps decreased the temptation to be a Sabbath breaker, the consequences for which were dire indeed (45). Except for the examples from Boston and Newport, Rhode Island, two seaport towns, the meetinghouses and early churches shown are from the kind of village described.

The Puritans who settled most of New England in the early seventeenth century sought the freedom to remove elaborate ceremonies and forms from their worship. The surviving meetinghouses are a tangible witness to this aim. The only ornamentation allowed, the elaborate pulpit and belfry (46, 47), was justified perhaps because they represented areas close to Heaven—a place of great beauty and richness in their thought. As Edmund Sinnott has written in describing Old South Church (41, 127):

> The steeple fits the building perfectly. The tower is as severe and
> unadorned as the rest of the meeting house, and all variety of design and
> beauty of ornament are saved until the eyes have traveled far aloft, almost
> as though the Puritan builder were tempting us to look upward from
> the barrenness of earth to the beauty of heaven.[6]

46 *View of pulpit in the Sandown Meetinghouse. (See 84.)*

47 *This woodcut, from the third edition of the children's book* The History of the Holy Jesus, *Boston, 1746, portrays Jesus preaching to the multitude. (A.A.S.)*

The secular function of the early meetinghouse, that of an assembly hall for the townspeople (48), insured its place as the most important building in the village. Here were held town meetings, and villagers heard proclamations on matters of general importance. At least one of the meetinghouses pictured, Pelham (118), has served this function since its very beginning.

Although too large to be called typical of seventeenth-century meetinghouses, Old Ship in Hingham, Massachusetts (49), has features often used late in the century. The frames were commonly of oak, with fitted joints pegged together. The frame was then planked and clapboarded on the outside and rough plastered inside. The frame remains visible along the walls and roof, although a plastered ceiling was added in some later buildings. The Hingham meetinghouse had a ceiling added about fifty years after it was built. The ceiling was removed recently, revealing again the beautiful framework of the loft. The meetinghouse was nicknamed "Old Ship" because of the loft's resemblance to an inverted ship's hull, the captain's walk on the roof, compass designs under the spire, and the pulpit's sounding board (50).

Two window levels allow light into the interior. The top row is at the level of the galleries located on three sides of the building. From the side opposite the middle or main entrance, the side without a gallery or entrance, rises the high

48   Town Meeting by E. Tisdale. Copper engraving, 1795. From M'fingal: A Modern Epic Poem, In Four Cantos by John Trumbull. (A.A.S.)
49, 50   See 1–5.

pulpit. Thus the minister (51) had a vantage point between two levels of listeners surrounding him on three sides. The exterior of larger examples of this early type of building is characterized by a roof that peaked from four sides to a balustrade and turret. The changing slope that makes a curve in the roof of the Old Ship is not typical of meetinghouses of this time. It is caused here by later enlargement of the building. The original 55′ x 45′ structure has been enlarged in two stages to 75′ x 55′.

Early in the eighteenth century, the often hip-roofed and square-dimensioned meetinghouse was followed by a style best illustrated by two examples in Brooklyn, Connecticut (52), and Amesbury, Massachusetts (53). Although both are much later than the earliest externally changed example, the Old South in Boston, in size and materials, the two smaller houses are more representative of the many that sprang up in New England during the century.

The exterior changes immediately apparent are the lengthening of sides, in contrast to the frequently square plan of the Old Ship type, and the use of a gable roof almost exclusively. When a belfry is needed, it now appears on top of a clearly stated, powerful tower which springs directly from the ground in the center of a shorter side. The main entrance, which may be through a porch of either one or two stories, is on a long side of the structure. The pulpit is opposite this entrance

51 Mr. Richard Mather *(1596–1669), Woodcut by John Foster (1648–1681). 1670. (A.A.S.)*
52 See *116, 124.*   53 See *37, 38, 39.*

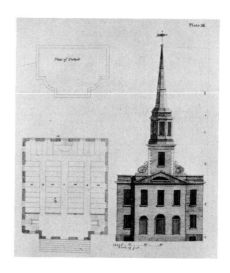

so that the galleries and the benches or box pews of the ground floor again surround the speaker—minister or town moderator—on three sides. Behind the pulpit is a window (54), similar in shape to many of the stones in the burial ground
adjacent to or near the meetinghouse. In the smaller structures, this is often the
only exterior element that shows it is not a dwelling of the period.

The early meetinghouses discussed thus far were established by Puritans or
Congregationalists. Until about 1800, the religion and government of New England
except for Rhode Island was Puritan. After the turn of the century, the union of
church and state was dissolved, and other denominations were tolerated under
the law. The design changes occurring near the end of the eighteenth century
in Congregational meetinghouses made them more like buildings of the Church
of England established in larger towns earlier in the century. Two such early
churches, Christ Church (Old North) in Boston, 1723, and Trinity Church in Newport, Rhode Island, 1725, if not actually designed by the English architect Chris-
topher Wren, are strongly influenced by the many churches he built in London
after the Great Fire of 1660. His followers and pupils, particularly James Gibbs,
wrote a number of builders' guides used by New England carpenters during the
last half of the century. A builders' handbook titled *The Country Builder's As-
sistant,* by a native New Englander, Asher Benjamin of Greenfield, Massachusetts,

54 Pulpit window from the Alna Meetinghouse. Maine. 1789.

55 Plate 38 from The American Builder's Companion of a New System of Architecture. *Asher Benjamin and David
Raynerd. Boston, 1806 (A.A.S.). See 100.*

and published in 1797, helped bring about a major change in meetinghouse design. The design in this and in later editions (55) was strongly influenced by English ideas as well as those of Boston architect Charles Bulfinch. The new buildings, now more properly called churches rather than meetinghouses, have undergone a change in seating plan so that the pulpit and entrance are at the opposite ends of the long axis of the building. The entrance is now through the tower end, turned to face the street. The tower itself is either absorbed into the body of the church so that it appears to begin on the roof (56) or begins as a porch or portico (e.g., the Bulfinch church in Lancaster, Massachusetts (16, 57). Increased acceptance of ornamentation is also apparent in Bulfinch's designs (58).

Receptiveness to style changes in architecture came about through events that radically altered the life of New Englanders. The separation from Great Britain by revolution led to experimentation with a new form of government. The new tolerance of people with other beliefs and aspirations, people who had different requirements for their places of worship, brought a change in the homogeneous character of towns and villages. New wealth allowed more time for leisure, education, and travel; young men like Bulfinch could travel in England and on the Continent. Exposure to contemporary European thinking and architectural monuments of the past profoundly affected the character of nineteenth-century America.

56   1802 Congregational Church. Windham, Vermont.
57   See 16, 17.   58   See 13.

The European (especially English) fascination with Classical Rome led to the rediscovery of the parent culture of Ancient Greece. In architecture, this enthusiasm was transmitted to the United States by English builders' manuals. The resulting style, the Greek Revival, lasting from about 1820 to the Civil War, dictated the form of most new church building as well as the inspiration for remodeling many older structures (59).

The transformation of the Greek temple into a New England church has often been surprisingly successful. The most obvious temple characteristic, the row of columns ringing the building, is used only on the church's facade. The colonnade may support a projecting pediment, forming a portico (60), or it may simply be a series of pilasters, flat vertical forms applied to the wall (61). With the notable exception of the Cathedral of St. Paul in Boston (14), a steeple is placed on the roof. This unexpected addition to the temple-inspired form can be successful if the designer is careful to relate the parts of the tower to the main structure. The stately Johnson Chapel at Amherst College accomplished this magnificently (15).

The Greek Revival, with all its apparent borrowings, still created an architecture with essentially similar qualities to that of the preceding 150 years. For a century, the hallmarks of early church architecture—simplicity, directness, and clarity—became dormant in New England religious building with few exceptions. It was overwhelmingly a time of eclecticism in architecture of all kinds, in Europe

59 1755 *Unitarian Church. Groton, Massachusetts. Remodeled 1839.*   60   *See 111.*
61 1799 *First Congregational Church. Ware, Massachusetts. Remodeled 1843.*

as well as in America. The way a great period of European church building, the Gothic, was re-created in America is described by Talbot Hamlin:

> In the Gothic Revival itself . . . there was an innate character which, developed, spelled the doom of the Greek [Revival]: that was its feeling — or rather its lack of feeling — for structure. To a much greater extent than with the Classic Revivals, the Medieval Revival had roots that were literary. Gothic romances led to "castellated" houses; in both it was the "atmosphere," the emotional effect, which was the essential thing. Naturally the way the effect was produced was secondary; the early Gothicists of America inevitably built effects rather than buildings. The whole cult of the picturesque was designed to disintegrate building techniques and lower building standards; if the result was a structure that was a good romantic picture, a pretty bit, what matter if its tracery was jigsaw wood, its battlements of boards?[7]

A European style even earlier than the Gothic, the Romanesque, became important in the 1870s through the influence of H. H. Richardson. His well-known early design (1877) for Trinity Church in Boston (62), although an undeniably intelligent ordering of great columns and complex surface details, has little

62 1877 Trinity Church. Episcopal. Boston, Massachusetts. Henry Hobson Richardson, architect.

relevance in a search for forms of lasting importance. In visual terms, it has not been able to withstand the onslaught of taller buildings that grew up around it. The exaggerated height of the tower and the richness of detail seem to demand that it be more important than the taller or plainer buildings around it. It seems doomed to perpetual conflict with its environment, while the simpler, more horizontal building facing it across Copley Square—McKim, Mead, and White's Boston Public Library (1888)—appears far better able to survive any future changes in its surroundings.

III. Twentieth-century religious architecture in New England no longer has the regional character of most of the early buildings. The present-day architect works in several widely separated sections of the country. Although many of the structures included here were designed by graduates of New England schools, a sizable number of the architects have roots elsewhere. New developments in heating technology and in materials have even made the vigorous climate a relatively minor concern. Finally, a very mobile population and instant communications, have produced a similar life style across the country.

Unfortunately, New England together with most of the country ignored the ideas of Frank Lloyd Wright, the most important of the few truly original American architects of the first half of the century. Wright's argument for an architecture

that developed naturally from its site, its purpose, local conditions, and from the nature of materials, recalls the way of early New England builders. His work did have considerable influence, however, on European architects at the cutting edge of the modern movement in the twenties. Modernists, like Walter Gropius and Ludwig Mies van de Rohe who emigrated to America in the late thirties, began to exert a powerful influence on American building after World War II through their teaching and practice.

Changes in liturgical practice have occurred simultaneously with the modern movement in architecture. The liturgical movement initiated by the Roman Catholic Church has had widespread implications for the congregation-clergy relationship. Its basic aim has been a closer union of clergy and worshipers. The changes in liturgy and architecture have been felt only in recent years in the United States. Although there were some interesting early experiments in this direction in New England—e.g., the circular Church of the Blessed Sacrament (63)—the forms enclosing new interior spaces have not always been successful. It is not uncommon to find a building with an elegant space formed by a hyperbolic paraboloid roof and curtained by totally unrelated walls. However, the structures pictured here show a total commitment to the new spirit of renewal in both religion and architecture. The possibilities inherent in new materials like reinforced con-

63 1954 *Church of the Blessed Sacrament. Roman Catholic. Holyoke, Massachusetts. Chester F. Wright, architect.*

crete and steel (64) are utilized in some, while in others we find a complete re-assessment and new application of old building staples — wood, brick, and stone.

> With the new materials, particularly steel and reinforced concrete, enabling the architect to break away from the narrow nave dictated by stone and wood, and with liturgical evolution developing in strong opposition to the Latin Cross plan, new and different concepts of ecclesiastic space are inevitably emerging. . . . It can well be argued that today there should be no pattern of church planning such as characterized the Romanesque, the Gothic, . . . and "Colonial." A church should grow from its particular requirements — its site, its climate, its neighbors, its program (65, 66, 67).[8]

That diverse demands are being met in the buildings chosen for this study is readily apparent when we examine two quite different churches by the same architect. Joseph J. Schiffer's Mt. Calvary Lutheran Church, Acton, Massachusetts (68), and, about thirty miles north in Andover, his Unitarian Universalist Church (69) offer striking solutions to their particular requirements.

The dark-wood Acton church seems to grow quite naturally from its level,

64 See 136, 137.   65 Church in the mountains of northern Italy.
66 1296–1462 Cathedral of Santa Maria del Fiore. Florence, Italy. Begun by Arnolfo di Cambio.

forested site. Glass visible from the exterior is kept to a minimum. The interior, however, is very well lighted by glass running the length of the truncated roof (6).

The Andover church, backed by a wooded area, is situated at the top of a small hill and the approach is through a large open field. The exposed concrete and glass structure complements or completes the landscape. Acting as a focal point, it draws the different spaces around it together. The homogeneous wooded character of the Acton site would have been disrupted by the contrasting elements of concrete and glass.

Perhaps the diametrically opposed theological views of the two congregations had even more force than the landscape in determining the forms of the Acton and Andover churches. The liberal, pragmatic approach of the Unitarian Universalist is revealed in the Andover church's complete dismissal of past solutions as valid for our time. Its basic shape is derived from one of the simplest three-dimensional shapes available to the designer, the cube. It suggests a conscious effort to lay aside all preconceived notions of what is "churchy."

The conservative Lutheran faith, with its clearly defined liturgy and tradition, has also been sympathetically understood. The architect has worked within guidelines that result in a structure not basically different from the earliest New England churches, particularly in the direct, clearly stated use of wood. Modern bonding

67 Seventeenth-century Church of Santa Maria della Salute along the Grand Canal in Venice, Italy.
68 See 6.   69 See 7.

techniques for wood, plywood, and laminated beams have been used masterfully to produce a very satisfying contemporary building.

The perceptive evaluation of church and site requirements combined with the necessary creative and technical ability to realize solutions are the factors that separate the architects' works illustrated here from the many others whose designs are not so successful.

In designing a chapel suitable for use by worshipers of all faiths at the Massachusetts Institute of Technology (71), Eero Saarinen chose as his starting point the elemental cylindrical form. The way he made the form live without destroying its essential simplicity reflects his careful consideration of every part. Because Saarinen's feelings and intentions for each part were conveyed so exactly to the builders, this viewer has the impression that the architect made the structure himself, brick upon brick.

It is interesting to speculate about some of Saarinen's unexpected formal devices. Is the moat around the building necessary? He apparently used this device to make the structure seem detached from its immediate surroundings — it is in another dimension, another world. This impression is reinforced by the entrance to the building through a long narthex over the moat (72). The bridgelike form, made of materials (glass and steel) unlike the main building, helps heighten the sense of entrance into a separate, mysterious space. The interior is lighted

70   *Tomb of Cecilia Metella, via Appia Antica, Rome, Italy. Tomb of the wife of one of Caesar's generals.*
71, 72   *See 106.*

from two sources—an intense white light from the round, honeycomb-grilled sky-light and a flickering, ethereal light reflected from the water in the moat along the lower circumference of the curved wall. The intense sunlight from the ceiling is led downward along a path of tiny suspended brass rectangles that lead to the altar (73). The result is a setting of great spirituality.

IV. In ending this study, it would be useful to highlight similarities between the early and contemporary buildings discussed. One of the striking similarities appears in repeated use of like forms arranged in a symmetrical pattern. In the old churches, windows are the strongest element working within planes created by walls. They are nearly always the same size and identically arranged around a central vertical axis. This symmetry also appears in elements placed upon the walls of new buildings. Usually the elements are glass, as in old churches, but patterns can also be created by other devices (74). Symmetry naturally results when order, unity, and simplicity are sought in design (75, 76).

The structures of both periods succeed because the builders understand the worshipers' needs. The early builder was usually a member of the community that made the building; the requirements of the congregation were also his require-ments. The responsibilities of the master builder of the past have been trans-ferred to the architect, a professional who understands the needs of many religious peoples.

73 See 107.   74 See 149.
75, 76 The "spirit" drawings are in the collection of the Hancock Shaker Village. See 29–33.

The heterogeneous makeup of our society has encouraged expanded use of synagogues and churches as community centers. The desire to perpetuate cultures from other lands, and to provide a setting for a distinct community, is strongly reminiscent of the religious and secular functions of the seventeenth- and eighteenth-century Puritan meetinghouse.

The liturgical changes that bring clergy and congregation in closer contact during worship have resulted in floor plans remarkably similar to those of Colonial churches. New floor-plan shapes — circular, elliptical, square — place the pulpit or altar nearer to the congregation, a design common not only in Colonial times but in the beginnings of the Christian church (77, 78).

Finally, contemporary forms have not been inspired by flights of fancy, or a desire to revive the glories of past civilizations. They have been a serious, direct answer to the needs of the contemporary society.

> The request that new buildings be stylistically contemporary is rooted in the nature of creativity and in the ethical principle of honesty. A creative act is normally born out of a cognitive and emotional participation in many or few creations of the past. But when the creative power of the artist or architect goes to work, it breaks through to the new, expressing the creator and through him his period. After a certain inevitable resistance and hesitation, his contemporaries come to recognize themselves in his work.[9]

77   *Portsmouth Priory Chapel. See 24–27.*

78   *522–547 Church of San Vitale. Ravenna, Italy. Guiliano Argentario (?), architect. The concentric positioning and progressive decreasing in size of the superstructures in these two buildings is an arrangement used often by designers of round or virtually round buildings. Compare 29, 103, 108.*

NOTES

(A.A.S.) has been used to credit the American Antiquarian Society of
Worcester, Massachusetts, who kindly granted permission to photograph the
early prints in their collection.

1. Sigfried Giedion, *Space, Time and Architecture* (Cambridge: Harvard
   University Press, 1963), p. xxxvii.
2. Joseph Rykwert, *Church Building* (New York: Hawthorn Books, 1966), p. 108.
3. G. E. Kidder Smith, *The New Churches of Europe* (New York: Holt, Rinehart
   and Winston, 1964), p. 13.
4. Ernest Short, *A History of Religious Architecture* (New York: W. W. Norton &
   Company, n.d.), p. 3.
5. Rykwert, *op. cit.,* p. 13.
6. Edmund W. Sinnott, *Meetinghouse and Church in Early New England* (New
   York: McGraw-Hill Book Company, Inc., 1963), p. 44.
7. Talbot Hamlin, *Greek Revival Architecture in America* (New York: Oxford
   University Press, 1944), p. 332.
8. Smith, *op. cit.,* p. 11.
9. Paul Tillich, "Contemporary Protestant Architecture," *Journal of the
   Liberal Ministry,* Vol. III, No. 1, Winter 1963.

In addition to the books cited above, the following were very useful in this project:

Downing, Antoinette F., and Scully, Vincent J., Jr., *The Architectural Heritage
   of Newport, Rhode Island,* 2nd revised edition (New York: Clarkson N. Potter,
   Inc., 1967).
Gowans, Alan, *Images of American Living* (Philadelphia and New York: J. B.
   Lippincott Company, 1964).
Lathrop, Elise, *Old New England Churches* (Rutland and Tokyo: Charles E. Tuttle
   Company, 1963).
Millar, John Fitzhugh, *The Architects of the American Colonies* (Barre,
   Massachusetts: Barre Publishers, 1968).
Rose, Harold, *Colonial Houses of Worship in America* (New York: Hastings
   House, 1963).

Apollo in the Democracy (New York: McGraw-Hill Book Co., 1968), p. 4.

In a long life I have become increasingly aware of the fact that the creation and love of beauty not only enrich man with a great measure of happiness but also bring forth ethical powers. — Walter Gropius*

80　1963　*Temple Beth Sholom. Manchester, Connecticut. Geddes, Brecher, Qualls, and Cunningham, architects.*
81　1962　*Temple Sinai. Stamford, Connecticut. Thomas A. Norton of Sherwood, Mills, and Smith, architect. Two quite different concepts of space enclosure are expressed by the prominent roofs. Temple Beth Sholom has a village-like arrangement of forms of varying size and importance that cluster around a dominant larger form, while Temple Sinai uses a single, hovering, all-encompassing shape to shelter its congregation.*

82 1962 Immanuel Lutheran
Church. Amherst, Massachusetts.
Olav Hammarstrom, architect.
The concrete arches above form
the side aisles.

83 1773–4 Sandown Meetinghouse. New Hampshire. One of the finest examples of its genre. Characteristic of the care shown throughout the structure are the front entrance doors. The side to the weather (far right) *is oak paneled, while the inside panels are natural pine to match the pine of the wainscoting and pews. The pulpit (46 in text) and the gallery wainscoting (84) are cherry. The wood columns and pilasters have been painted to simulate marble.*

17

84 *View of the box pews and the gallery that the minister or town moderator has from the Sandown pulpit. The closeness of pulpit to benches is typical of meetinghouses until the end of the eighteenth century. Twentieth-century religion finds this proximity agreeable and is experimenting with various arrangements to achieve it.*

85 *On the following pages is an enlarged detail of one of the gallery staircases shown here.*

*86   c. 1770 German
Lutheran Meeting House.
Waldoboro, Maine. Yellow
with white trim.*

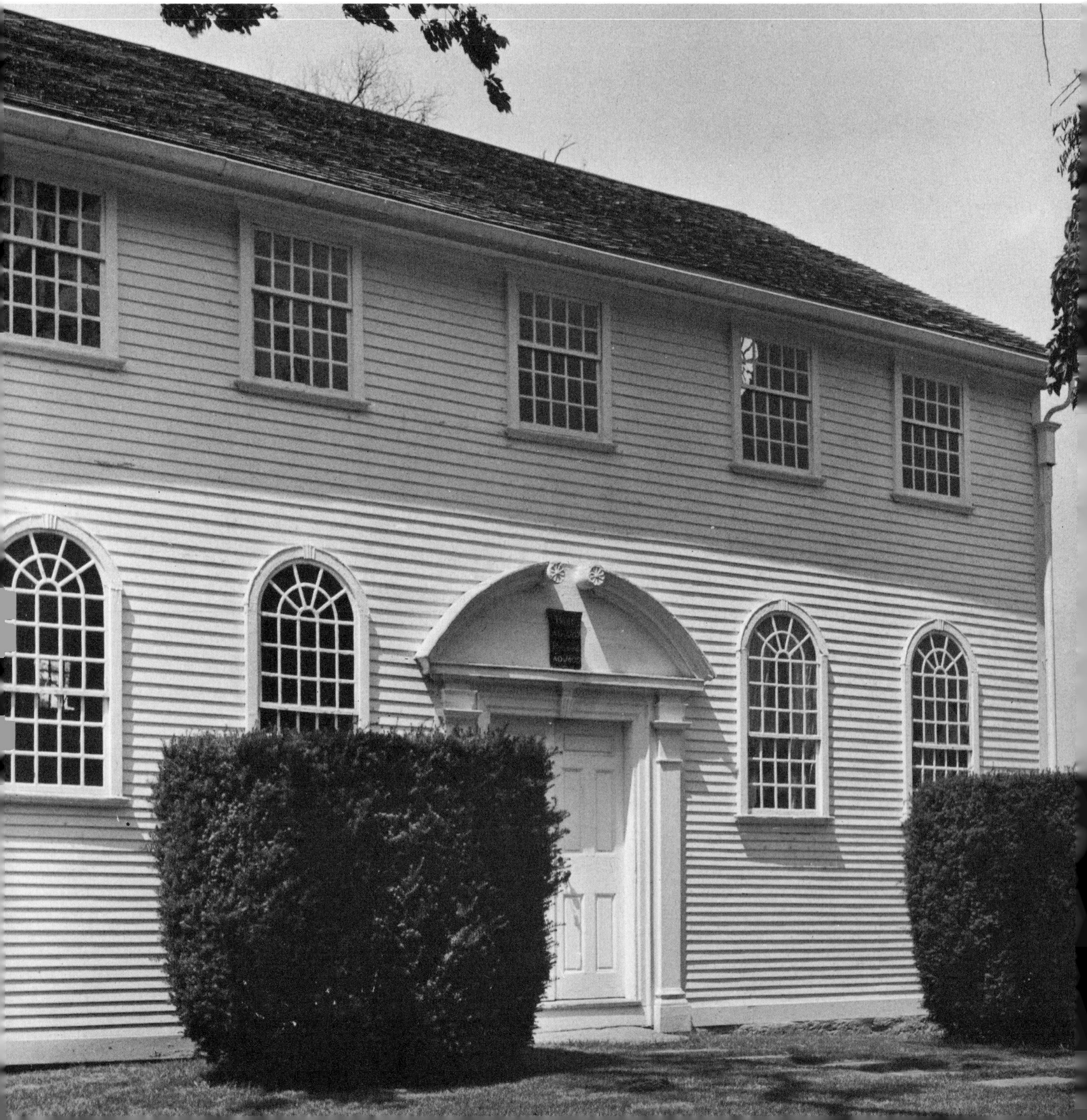

87 1707 *St. Paul's Church (Old Narragansett Church). Anglican. Wickford, Rhode Island.*

88 1810 *Friends Meetinghouse. East Sandwich, Massachusetts.*

89 1787 *Rockingham Meetinghouse. Vermont.*

90 1769 *Chestnut Hill Meetinghouse. Millville, Massachusetts.*

92   1786 *East Hoosac Friends Meetinghouse. Adams, Massachusetts.*

93 1969 Lutheran Church, Berlin, Connecticut. Richard E.
Schoenhardt of Galliher and Schoenhardt, architect.

94 1966 Church of the Messiah. Episcopal. Foster, Rhode Island. William D. Warner, architect.

95   1963   *Westminster Unitarian Church. East Greenwich, Rhode Island. William D. Warner, architect.*

96   1957   *Chapel of St. James the Fisherman. Episcopal. Wellfleet, Massachusetts. Olav Hammarstrom, architect.*

97

98

97   *Detail of the Wellfleet Chapel's belfry and spire.*

98   *1820 detail of the Unitarian Church. Mendon, Massachusetts. Elias Carter, architect.*

99 1816 Unitarian Church. Bedford,
Massachusetts.

100 Plate 39 from The American Builder's
Companion by Asher Benjamin. Boston. 1806.
(A.A.S.) Asher Benjamin's design for Old West
Church in Boston, which is reproduced as one of
the two church plans in his 1806 edition of The
American Builder's Companion, was most likely the
inspiration for the unknown builder of the Bedford
Church. Benjamin may in turn have been
influenced by Charles Bulfinch's design for the
New North Church (St. Stephen's, 15).

101, 102 (overleaf) Plates 98 and 86 from The
Builder's Jewel by Batty Langley. 1800. (A.A.S.)
This book was first published in London in 1741.
Langley (1696–1751) was an English architect and
architectural writer.

100

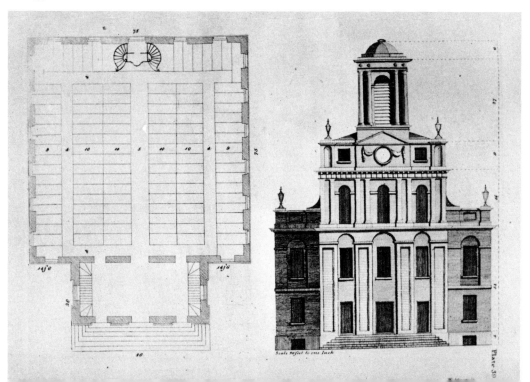

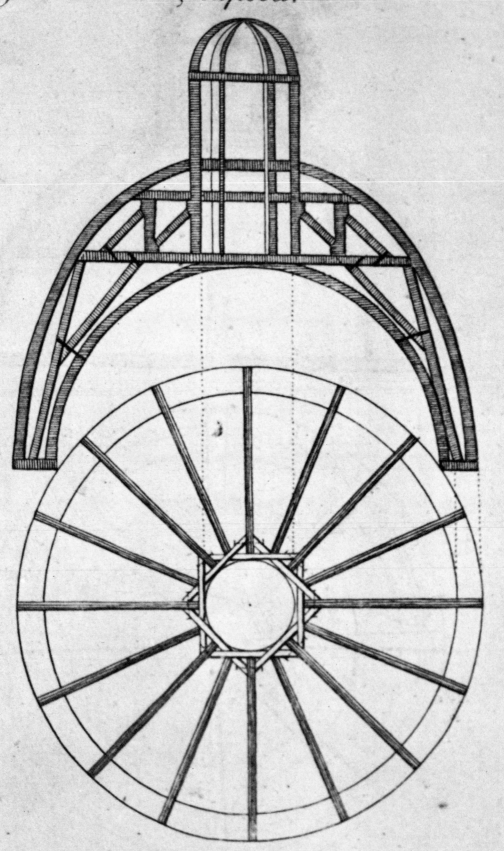

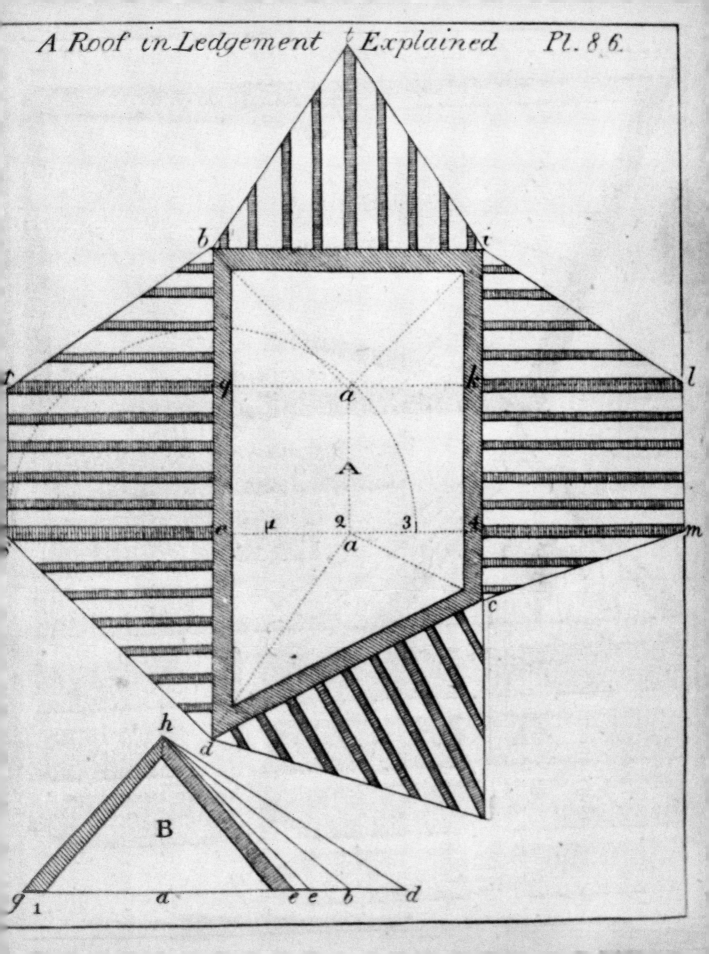

103　1967　Pierce Chapel, Cranwell School. Roman Catholic. Lenox, Massachusetts. Peter McLaughlin, architect. The elliptical structure is of concrete and glass. The stained glass and the glass/aluminum spire are the work of Joseph Ferguson.

104 1962 United Church of Rowayton,
Connecticut. Joseph Salerno, architect. This
shell-like form is situated in a small coastal village.

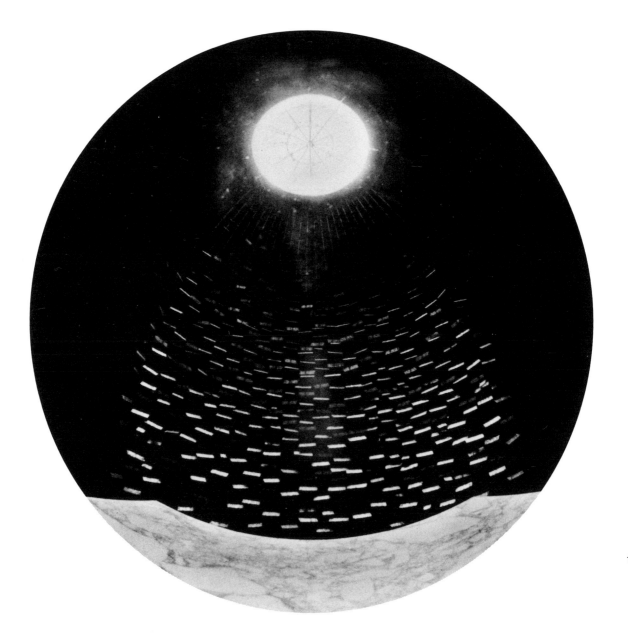

105 *Seventeenth century. Newport Tower. Rhode Island.*

106 *1954. Kresge Chapel, Massachusetts Institute of Technology. Cambridge.*
Eero Saarinen and Associates, architects. Aluminum spire by sculptor
Theodore Roszak.

107 *A fish-eye view from the top surface of the altar to the skylight, following the path of the brass*
screen designed by Harry Bertoia.

The MIT Chapel, which seemed in the 50s so unprecedented a form, has much in common with earlier structures for both religious and secular use. Even in limiting our survey to New England and the buildings in these pages, we can discover several intriguing early circular structures. In addition to the "Old Round Church" in Vermont (108) and the round Shaker barn (29), perhaps the most arresting in relation to the chapel is the mysterious round stone tower in Newport. Its origin has been much discussed. The most fascinating suggestion: it was a place of worship built by Norsemen some seven centuries ago. However agreeable this possibility seems, most archaeological and historical research points to the less romantic probability that it is the remains of a mill built by Governor Benedict Arnold, who bought the land on which it stands sometime after 1650. Comparison with a woodcut of a mill of the same period is quite revealing. (45) Origin and use notwithstanding, it is interesting to see how similarly the walls have been opened up on the upended cylinders that form the old mill and the Saarinen chapel. The arches maintain the essential simplicity of the cylinder form, avoiding the blank impression the shape would otherwise have on this grand scale.

108 *1813 Old Round Church. Richmond, Vermont. Erected jointly by five*
denominations—Congregational, Baptist, Universalist, Methodist, and Christian,
the building has 16 sides.

109 *1730 First Baptist Church (Clapboardtrees Meetinghouse). Originally*
Congregational. Westwood, Massachusetts. Belfry c. 1835.

110   Washington, New Hampshire. (Left) Washington Congregational Church. 1840. (Right) Old Meetinghouse. 1789; now the Town Hall. Tower c. 1800. Between the two stands the Central School. On one of the highest elevations in a sparsely populated section of New Hampshire stands this exquisite grouping of buildings. The unity of the town center has been achieved without sacrificing the uniqueness of its several parts.

111   Meriden, Connecticut. (Left) First Baptist Church. 1848. (Right) Center Congregational Church. 1830.

112   1827   Arnold Mills Methodist Church. Rhode Island.

113   1760   Danville Meetinghouse. New Hampshire. The simplicity of window design in the meetinghouses of this period recalls a statement made by Mary McCarthy in The Stones of Florence about Florentine architect Brunelleschi's windows: ". . . [the windows] are a plain statement of the notion 'window,' cut out of a wall with a terse finality that makes other windows appear haphazard accidents or bellicose rhetoric in comparison."

114   1774   Kensington Congregational Church. Connecticut. The belfry was added and interior changes made in 1837.

115   1775   Old Meetinghouse. Jaffrey Center, New Hampshire. Tower c. 1820.

116   1770   Old Meetinghouse. Unitarian since 1819. Brooklyn, Connecticut. Interior now being restored to its original condition. It should be noted that the proposal to build this new meetinghouse, to replace the earlier house on this site, started the controversy between the Congregationalists and the wealthy landowner Godfrey Malbone that resulted in the building of Trinity Church (8) in Brooklyn. As an important taxpayer, Anglican Malbone was required to pay a large part of the cost of the new meetinghouse unless he belonged to another church in the town. Malbone decided to organize an Episcopal parish with several other families in the area. Their building, Trinity Church, was completed a few months before the meetinghouse, thus exempting Malbone from paying a tax for the Congregational structure. Understandably, Trinity differs in design from the typically handsome Congregational meetinghouse. Its exterior has much in common with Peter Harrison's design for Touro Synagogue (9) in Newport. Since Malbone had only recently arrived from his native Newport, the fledgling designer predictably turned to a familiar building for inspiration.

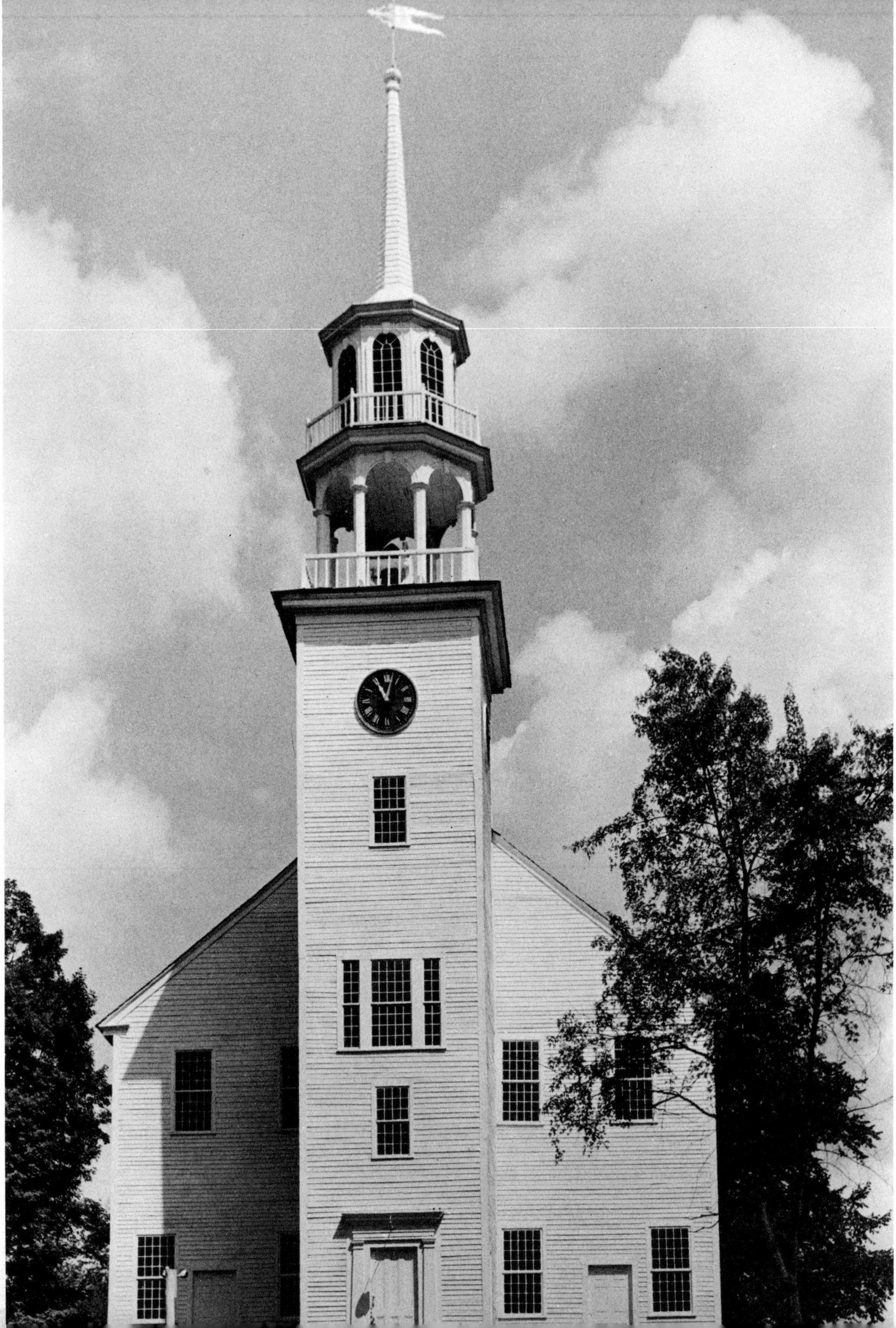

117 1799 *Old Meetinghouse. Strafford, Vermont.*

118 1743 *Old Meetinghouse. Pelham, Massachusetts. Functioning
continously as a town hall since first built.*

119 1796 *Congregational Church. Rindge, New Hampshire.*

120 1771 *Old Meetinghouse. Townsend, Massachusetts.
Congregational, Unitarian, and, since the 1850s, Methodist.
Tower c. 1800.*

121   1771   Townsend Methodist Church. Tower c. 1800.

122   1717   West Parish Meetinghouse. West Barnstable, Massachusetts.

123   1799   Old Meetinghouse. Strafford, Vermont.

124   1770   Old Meetinghouse. Brooklyn, Connecticut.

125   1775   Old Meetinghouse. Jaffrey Center, New Hampshire. Tower c. 1820.

*126   1747   First Parish Meetinghouse. Unitarian. Cohasset, Massachusetts.
Tower c. 1800.*

127   1729   Old South Meetinghouse. Boston, Massachusetts.

128   1723   Old North Church (Christ Church). Boston, Massachusetts.

*129   1771   Congregational Church. Farmington, Connecticut. Judah Woodruff,
builder.*

*130   1726   Trinity Church. Anglican. Newport, Rhode Island. Richard Munday,
builder.*

*131   1769   First Church Congregational. Originally Presbyterian. East Derry, New
Hampshire. Tower 1824.*

132   1789   Old Meetinghouse. Washington, New Hampshire. Tower c. 1800.

133   1761   First Church of Christ. Congregational. Wethersfield, Connecticut.

The towers in this series are unique in that they can be seen in their entirety. Usually the tower is
either a partially seen, pilaster-like form or appears to begin on the roof. The clearly articulated,
projected towers here, rather than being an appendage to the main form, are perceived as one of the
two geometric shapes that make up the whole structure. The counterpoint played by the vertical
tower to the horizontal box form of the church, is reminiscent of the silo-barn relationship on farms.
Since many of the remaining New England working farms are in remarkable harmony with their
environment and a joy to look at, the church-barn analogy is used in the most complimentary sense.

133

134, 135   1958   First Presbyterian
Church. Stamford, Connecticut.
Wallace K. Harrison, Harrison and
Abramovitz, architect. Tower 1968.

135 Thousands of chunks of colored glass have
been embedded into the precast
reinforced-concrete shell.

139   1967   *Church of the Cross. Lutheran.*
Hanover, Massachusetts. Joseph J. Schiffer,
architect.

140   1967   *Christ the King Lutheran Church.*
Nashua, New Hampshire. Olav Hammarstrom,
Bednarski and Stein, associated architects.

141 1967 Trinity Episcopal Church. Rockland,
Massachusetts. Joseph J. Schiffer, architect.

142   *Two of the approximately 2500 granite*
blocks, each 9.5' x 3.5', used in the construction
of the monastery.

143   1970 *Carthusian Charterhouse. Manchester, Vermont. Victor Christ-Janer, architect. Same wall from two*
viewpoints.

The monastery for the ancient Carthusian order is placed high on a shoulder of Mt. Equinox in southern Vermont. The
impressive size (500' x 700'), the emphasis on permanence, the beautiful, remote location, the strict, austere life
of the inhabitants, place it as one of the more notable monuments of religion in this country.

143

144   1963 Phoenix Mutual Life Insurance Co., Hartford, Connecticut.
Harrison and Abramovitz, architects.

145   1955 Berlin Chapel, Brandeis University. Waltham, Massachusetts.
Harrison and Abramovitz, architects.

The office building, by the firm that designed the chapel, seems to play a role in its urban site not unlike that of a successful religious structure. The Phoenix building, which has evolved from the form of the chapel, i.e., the curved side walls of the earlier form being continued until they meet, has a spiritual presence. The building depends upon the extreme simplicity of its unexpected shape, the insistent repetition of the tinted window walls and structural members, the reflected patterns on the walls, and the intense feeling of verticality, to create a transcendent atmosphere reminiscent of the cathedral form in a medieval town. The view from the north of this jewel-like structure — seemingly detached and a focus for the many taller buildings in the Hartford skyline — is an uncommon visual experience.

144

145, 146   1955 Interfaith Center. Brandeis University. Waltham, Massachusetts. Harrison and Abramovitz, architects. From left: Berlin Chapel (Jewish), Bethlehem Chapel (Catholic), and Harlan Chapel (Protestant).

147 1965 Mount Zion Seventh-Day Adventist Church. Hamden, Connecticut. Earl Carlin,
architect. This church of concrete blocks illustrates emphatically that even unimposing
materials can be successful in the hands of an imaginative designer.

148 1965 Congregation Agudath Sholom.
Stamford, Connecticut. Lewis Davis, Davis
and Brody, architect.

148

149 1964 *Temple Anshe Amunim.
Pittsfield, Massachusetts. Henry L.
Blatner, architect. The sanctuary,
enclosed in the center of the
structure, is lighted by a large,
circular dome. The Hebrew charac-
ters on the front, meaning "People
of Faith" (Anshe Amunim), by
L. Hirsche. See 74.*

150   *Cathedral of the Pines. Rindge, New Hampshire.*

*A view of New England meetinghouses would
be incomplete without including stones from
eighteenth-century churchyards. The exaggerated
monumentalism of much recent memorial art is
missing in these slender slate markers. The
simplicity in the carving of the faces and decorative
symbols shows an instinctive understanding of
material and design that often results in sculpture
of great sincerity and beauty.*

*151   1758 Old Meetinghouse. Harpswell Center,
          Maine. The gravestones included are
          from several locations.*

In Memory of
Silas Whitcomb
ſon of Lieut Aſa &
Mrs Sarah Whitcomb
who died April 9th
1795, aged 7 years,
6 months & 18 days

In Memory of
Reuben Hunt, Son of
Lieut Reuben Hunt and
Mrs Rebekah his wife,
who died Febr ye 18th
AD 1777 Aged 3 Years.

Say lovely, prattling, playful boy,
Thy Father's hope, thy Mother's joy,
Why didst thou make so short a stay,
But steal our hearts, & then away,
God gives & takes, let man adore,
Death waits me to th' immortal shore.

Here lies Buried the Body
of Mr David Wheeler

In Memory of
Mrs SARAH CURTIS
Wife of Mr TIMO CURTIS
Died May 6th 1784
Aged 46 Years

In memory of

Enſign David Day

who died June 17th 1792

in the 84th year.

Here lies the Body
of Sally Hall
Daughter of Mr
John Hall & Mrs
Sarah his wife the
died Aug 24 1778